Up, up and Away

George Sfougaras

Copyright

Contents

Prologue

Short Stories of travel, longing, and hope. Sometimes funny, sometimes not so much.

Here I am attempting to write a little book of short stories and observations. I make it sound as if I just stumbled across this process, a bit like a lucky accident. It is not really thus, for this little collection has taken years to gather. I am grateful to myself for having the foresight to write down things as they were happening. It is such a powerful thing: Immediacy; the moment; the present. When it becomes the past, nice as it still is, it gets a little fuzzy. Our mind adds things, embellishes, and forgets. I wrote these short 'stories' whilst I was in the moment. A bit like a declaration of love. Nice when it comes a few days later in a beautiful letter, but, so much more powerful when screamed out in the moment whether on a helter-skelter or in another context which I will leave to your imagination.

George Sfougaras 2023

One

Airports

Airports. Such fun. I always associated air travel with a certain élan, in a '60s James Bond kind of way. Ladies in large Sophia

Loren sunglasses and impeccable manners. Greying gentlemen smelling of Vetiver and pipe tobacco, carrying a little valise of essentials... perhaps a misunderstood spy or two.

Of course, but of course, the reality is somewhat different. A loud scratching PA system streams an incomprehensible array of white noise at a sweaty, post-euphoric crowd, comprising many young folk of all genders and sensibilities, with incredibly symmetric eyebrows. Some are dressed to impress, and it is impressive that some have managed to get dressed. Many, encouraged by the shrill background noise are also shouting loudly. Some have no fear of germs and suchlike and are sitting, lying eating, and sleeping on a floor laid when marble was cheap. The little canteen is making enough to pay back a significant part of the national debt. Only large expensive bottles of water are available.

The flight has been delayed.

They can't process us quickly enough.

Two

The Captain

The captain of our airplane is a woman. I find that hugely reassuring. I have come to expect that if a woman is in charge, things will simply run better and safer.

I have also started to think that since men pilots stopped appearing in cigarette adverts alongside unfeasibly manicured admirers of fag smoke, or as heroic characters in disaster movies, being a pilot is no longer a male fantasy, but ranks alongside veterinarian science as a career choice. Marvelous being a vet, amazing for sure, but, you know, it is slightly less photogenic than piloting. I think that the perceived loss of poseur power has discouraged a certain demographic from applying to attend pilot school.

Our aforementioned womanly pilot stepped out of the cockpit (shouldn't that be the henpit?) to reassure us as we sat on the plane waiting for a 'window' to take off. Using incomprehensible but impressive terminology such as 'apron', 'hopping on' and reassuring us that Brussels was aware of our predicament had limited impact. As soon as the French air control was mentioned obliquely as the possible 'source of the problem', however, a knowing murmur rose uniformly from the cabin. The French. Of course. Now everyone sat back and relaxed. The French and their 'funny ways' nodded sagely the mature gentleman in the seat opposite. A few passengers shook their heads. 'The French'. They were responsible. Everything made sense again. Suddenly waiting became a show of maturity. 'We'll show (them) how grown up we are'.

The captain cut an incredibly swish figure as she addressed us. Sharp as something that epitomizes sharpness as a concept, pin? knife? razor? She stood sideways like an archer taking aim, her head looking over her right shoulder and speaking into the microphone. She spoke clearly in a way that made me feel that this pilot knew best. Male pilots always make me think that they have forgotten something... like refueling, for instance. I had to shake the childish thought that she might at any moment 'turn' and have me standing in the corner wearing a pointy hat with a big D on it.

Soon after the 'apron' became available (a bit of the airstrip apparently) Brussels gave us the nod and Captain Fabulous pulled that throttle, or something, and catapulted us into the fluffy clouds. We all sat back happy that Brussels had seen our side and that 'the French' had not won this one. We proceeded to ascend victoriously to the appropriate height. Our pilot occasionally spoke and a surprising silence fell upon us each time. Pilot knows best after all, and flying is as safe as houses again.

Three

Part of the Journey

I used to love airports. There, I could blend in, another exotic foreigner globe-trotting, a rich, interesting citizen of the world, (probably) embarking on a fabulous adventure. I have written before of the wonderful romanticism that travel always held for me. Mystery and a sense of endless possibilities evoked the essence of Aladdin, James Bond, Thomas Cook and Marco Polo. (All men). The women were the cause of the travel, muses, beloved, lost loves, and exotic destinations for a male ego stinking to high heaven of Brut or High Karate. Maybe cigar smoke, possibly Brylcream, or extra strong mints. Ready for any occasion, the lonely (for the time being) seasoned traveler smelling of synthetic aromatic concoctions, ever ready for that elusive kiss, despite his poor 1970s dental hygiene, would shuffle his way through oriental markets, arid deserts and secret caves of wonder. It was a cheap teenage fantasy (with some cynical elements thrown in through a revisionist lens) untrue then and even more so now.

I am sitting opposite a young couple and the young woman's mother. There has been an 'accident' involving the 'f******g' boyfriend's water. The *s******g' bag is gone to 's***t'. This 'f********g' holiday was a 'w******s' idea. The said accident necessitates the emptying of the aforementioned 'f******g' bag and urgent wiping of each item that has not rolled on the floor. The waiting room seats are arranged in rows which makes such minor dramas easily viewable by hundreds of people. The acoustics are also excellent so that all the expletives are clearly heard by the numerous children watching. I secretly wish that our local theatre provided such exemplary views and sound. I often struggle to see past the gentleman's head in the row in front of me, but here, I am almost an actor in the play. The mother's posterior is helpfully pushing my luggage towards the gate as she genuflects to collect the errant items off the floor. The young woman is texting in an effort to calm herself down, I presume. Her iPhone screen flexes under angry fingers. I imagine many an f**** forming on the shiny display. I hope there is no emoticon for the aforesaid verb.

The boyfriend is munching on his bacon cob (a mere £4.99 without sauce) from the airport 'deli'. I unpack a new set of earphones. My phone battery is flagging, so I just shove them in airtight to drown the swearing. My flight is announced as delayed by an hour on the overhead display screen. I clutch my cross and begin a desperate murmured prayer. I think rocking a little on the spot might help. I get some strange looks. That's okay, it's all part of the journey.

Four

The Artistry of a Good Haircut

(And the misery of a bad one).

Up until the age of 21, no one ever cut my hair apart from my father. I was reminded of the fact yesterday when one of my daughters posted a photograph of a horse, whose mane had been clipped in a very straight line. This was a comment on my hairdressing skills, not my dad's. When the girls were little, I used to cut their fringes, and the horse picture was a reminder of my one and only style, the geometric hairdo. My father, on the other hand, was a skilled barber and hairdresser.

A ten-year-old orphaned Christian boy, he was taken in as a shop helper by a Muslim barber in 1920s Istanbul and learned a trade that he knew would give him an income to support himself and his baby brother. He graduated to having his own salons and teaching at the Kamer Institute in Athens. So, he could cut hair. I was always guaranteed a great haircut, always effortless and he really understood my coarse and unruly mop.

His passing was far sadder than anything else I had experienced until then, and now, four decades after his death, it seems like only yesterday, when he would patiently clip away and make me look human again when the clump of black wiry hair on my little head grew to ridiculous proportions.

My childhood hair, encouraged by the daily swims in the sea, the dust, and the rough and tumble of growing up at a time when we were pretty much allowed to spend all day running and falling over, would silently fall on the floor; black puffs and wiry wool clumps, and in the mirror two faces, both smiling. But why the build-up? Today, I looked in the mirror, a mere week after an unfortunate haircut. What a joyless thing is a bad haircut! What an annoyance and a reminder of one's petty intolerances, really. My life has not been drastically affected by having this cut. I have not suffered loss of sleep, it has not made me sad, and I have not wished the barber ill. But, all the same, I think of him every day.

I look in the mirror and I see the badly shorn angles on my temples. I desperately pat down the disproportionate quiff that is making me look slightly ridiculous at my age. I recall him snipping away without proper focus. And I feel sorry for him. How awful it must be to not be able to do a job well. Of course, lots of us do jobs badly, some of the time. I want to be magnanimous. A lot of us make mistakes. Not like this, surely. He cuts hair every day. Is he always this bad? If you do the same drawing again and again and you never improve, what would you do? It is hard to have perspective when it comes to our own outcomes and I think cutting hair must be one of those cases of simply not being aware of your own errors.

To generalise somewhat, in many barbers' shops, there are usually a couple of people cutting hair. The owner and an apprentice. The owner is the older chap and has learned to cut hair the old way: scissors and a comb. Hands, usually old hands, glide effortlessly. His talk is normally quiet, a bit more thoughtful. He has seen it all, heard it all. He paces the cut. He holds up the mirror and there is his handy work. Clean, not exciting, but accurate. The younger man has 'done' a BTEC. The electric clippers are his tool of choice. Buzzing and laughing about his weekend exploits and his planned purchase of a large motorbike, he will let his wayward hand fly around your head, sometimes hitting the target, at other times nonchalantly carving out a sad little groove of hair. Steps and little uneven patches are his trademarks.

The thinning scissors are a real giveaway. When they are waved around with gay abundon, you know you will suffer. This tool is amazing and in the right hands makes thick hair more manageable. In the wrong hands, however, it simply creates the impression of natural hair loss. Little spaced-out square teeth will cut randomly and accidentally where they should not. *Et voila!* A product may be hastily applied to style the ensuing mess. 'Great', I quip as I look at the nest of badly arranged gel on my tired, lined face. 'Great'. The real damage is only discernible in its full glory, after a shampoo.

This morning, there it was again. I am not used to thinking about people I do not really know well. But darn it! I have been forced to think of the barber every time I have looked in the mirror. I think of him with a kind of annoyance but also disbelief. Is it that hard to cut hair? He does it every day. Does everyone feel as let down as me? Do people actually complain? Let's be honest. I usually circle the shop to make sure that the guy who can actually cut hair is free. He seldom is. When there is a likelihood that I may be caught out and have to settle for the apprentice, I will probably walk on and come back another time.

There is something very embarrassing about walking into a barber's and waiting for one of them to finish and do your hair, whilst, in the meantime, the apprentice is playing with his phone. So timing is of the essence. You just have to jump in, just as the chair of the master is freed up from the last customer and not before.

If you, as I did, mistime your entry, you are doomed.

Doomed.

Five

'Chase a Crooked Shadow'

I am watching what feels like a typical B-movie: 'Chase a Crooked Shadow'. I have the volume turned down low. I have no idea what it is about. It is late. It is on a channel called 'Talking Pics'; I am not really watching it, as such. It is on in the background as I look through some art therapy ideas, as bedtime reading is replete and I am in need of alternatives. There is some dysfunctional, gender biased, awkward 1950s romantic tension thing trying to happen. A good woman. A bad man. His eyes betray him, shifting and narrowing intermittently.

The director has told him to "shift them like crazy." I imagine a Greek accent (Elia Kazan?). Although the film is not really in the same league as Kazan's work. He obeys. He is shifting them. Left to right, back again... and again. He faces the camera, responding to her words, while her face is visible behind his shoulder. He heads the bill. A 50s heartthrob in a pullover, with sleeves, neatly folded over his biceps, not bunched up, presumably to accentuate his manly arms. Instead, he looks odd.

I imagine past the black and white footage the colour of the jumper to be canary yellow. He looks sweaty but his arms are well-ventilated. He lights up. A cigarette appears from an invisible packet. He is adept at lighting up. Years of practice. Those long sticks of compacted tobacco shreds. He expertly pops one in between thin lips. Petrol lighter at hand. A smooth hand movement from the trouser pocket (below the camera line) to the mouth, to ignite that flimsy tobacco-stuffed tube. He breathes in. DNA-altering chemicals are sucked in. He exhales. It is a thick cloud of particles laden with moisture. He is cool apparently. Smoking was cool.

I am back to my notes, but look up at the TV. His eyes shift, and he inhales and exhales. When the camera stops filming, he will light up another. Everyone will light up with him. Hell, the whole film crew are probably smoking as they work. As they eat, whilst driving. In the bath; in bed. The film is in black and white. The actor looks as if he is in his late 30s. It was 1958 when the film was made. He is not with us anymore. We watch him. He breathes out. In the next scene, he is thankfully back in a black suit, but still smoking. I think about art. Art with purpose.

Whilst this is playing out, I am struggling with my own much more immediate issues. The act of making. Making stuff that I consider important. I reproach myself. All acts of making, no, not just making, all acts have meaning. I am not going to attribute value or create a hierarchy. It could end up messy. Making art as important as breathing, contemplating the meaning of life compared to the intrinsic value of smoking... erm... not so easy. It is enough to wrestle with one's own life and find meaning in the acts that one commits to. All the same, I am making a personal choice, a judgment in terms of my own outcomes. And yes, it is a compulsion, this wanting to create a 'meaningful' narrative, to make a piece of work into a story worth telling. It seems almost ludicrous. Surely we can make stuff just for the fun of it?

These internal conversations of mine always end up the same. With a 'Yes, but...'. Trying too hard can kill a story, like pulling up a seedling to make sure it is taking root. So while he smokes, I agonize. The mind wanders. My story, like smoke, drifts up and stains the wallpaper. Another impasse. Tomorrow will be easier, surely. In the light of day, these things these conundrums, usually evaporate.

The next day I find out a bit more about the film and feel guilty as being critical of the director and the cast. It is a big deal making anything and they really had a good go at it. Of course, my questions are still there.

Six

The Dream

I recall with immense sadness my parents' regrets after they sold their home in Greece. I believe that they felt it more acutely than they let on. They regretted leaving their country, they were too old to change, and 1970s England was far bleaker than a couple in their 60s could have imagined. It was a difficult time. The junta's grip on the country had exacerbated the old wounds left by the Civil War. Dad was a socialist and it must have hurt him to witness such a turn towards the right. Mum kept telling him to be quiet because speaking his mind was dangerous. Hard to imagine now, the beatings, the disappearances the state-sanctioned violence. Ultimately, they left for us, their children. My sister had married an English engineer and I had come to be with them and started attending secondary school. My brother was doing his national service in the Greek army, and we imagined that he would eventually join us. It seemed that being together as a family was more important than their comfort, their country, their way of life. I shudder now when I think of the leap of faith they took. The subsequent hardship they endured, and the enormity of their loss.

Their longing for a return home became stronger until the sadness of it took my father. He cared too much, that's my unqualified diagnosis. Loss poisoned him, silenced him. But it never took away his smile, and his hugs although weaker, stayed warm, daily, reassuring. I loved him and I loved looking after him, with my tireless mum. I am grateful for them every day. In the years preceding his illness, he had traveled back to Crete a few times looking for a house. It was not meant to be. The universe had other plans...

That is why, years later, I continued the search with my wonderful partner, and together, we managed to make that dream come true. My parents' faded photograph is in a small stone nook inside the small village house. It was remarkably easy in some ways because we wanted it to happen. Keeping that dream alive, and going back yearly has been the challenge. Leaks, water damage, mould, the outcomes of our prolonged absence through Covid, illness, and life circumstances have played their part.

Life in the village far from the city would have been unfamiliar to my parents who ran a business in Herakleion. Still, it is the land, the roof, the house, the part of the old home country, that now belongs to them again. We are temporary, ephemeral yet we long for this ownership, this stewardship of the ground beneath our feet. A corner of the Earth we can truly call home. To me, it is a sacred right, this keeping of a thing whose life span surpasses our brief human lives. The custody of a dream is twice the dream.

I have trouble believing in an afterlife. I feel happier at the prospect of eternal rest, but I can't help wishing that somehow, they know they have a home in their country once more. Outside the little house, I have painted its name: Mikro Kastro. (Little Castle). Kastro is also another name for Herakleion, where they spent most of their lives.

Seven

The Quiet Village

You would think that living in an isolated spot somewhere in the mountains, in a village of less than 400 souls, would afford one a level of privacy which is not possible in the cramped Victorian Terraces of the English inner city. You would, of course, be wrong. Privacy is diminished by an interest in people, that frankly is non-existent in colder climes. People remember your face. Your name. What you do. You may quickly acquire a nickname, which describes you to others in a place where everyone knows everyone.

They say that sometimes you can hear a large village before you see it! Greek village life is not designed with quiet, or privacy in mind. It is a communal affair where, due to the limited exposure to other entertainment, people are still seen as 'interesting'. The layout of the streets and the general planning, such as it is, is not meant to separate people but to bring them together.

Houses face each other across narrow streets and the little roads are often an extension of someone's house. It is almost impossible to get through a village in the summer evenings, without greeting someone or stopping to talk - but then, why would you?

Then there are a surprising number of itinerant salesmen in trucks and four-by-fours, selling everything from watermelons to fresh fish. They, depending on their daily route, can arrive before eight and blast you out of your slumber with their loudspeakers. Local farmers in four-by-fours also come and go at various times, with whatever produce their fields or allotments have yielded.

There are communal rituals, festivals, the making of *raki*, in November, Christmas and the long Easter preparations, religious observances, and the final great feast at the end of the Holy Week; St. Mary's in August, with the great Glendi (fiesta) on the 15th August, the deafening church bells that ring out repeatedly every Sunday (from 8 am) and dozens of important Saint-days (each day has a particular saint of saint or religious event, but luckily they are not all celebrated with the same aplomb).

The gathering of flowers on the 1st of May, making wreaths for the doors to welcome in the spring, then at the end of May burning the dried wreaths and jumping over the flames. If you like occasions and you want to be a part of a community, village life is for you. Villages vary of course, from the almost deserted, to those which are like small towns, so choose carefully.

There are the greetings to the neighbours, cockerels every dawn and early afternoon, the occasional donkey braying, goats bleating, dogs barking, and of course the cats. Sometimes a weasel is loudly chased away, and at times a walking stick is thrown at the poor creature and bounces on the cobbled street clattering behind it as it skedaddles to the nearest ditch.

I was looking at a weasel pass by a cat and marveled at how they differ. Although cute, weasels lack the social skills of the cats and their cuddly looks. Cats are the masters of the cute and their manner and appearance are somehow designed to please us, engage us in an exchange, make us feel pity, or sacrifice a bit of kebab; in the case of tourists staying for a brief time, a regular supply of cat food. Should you be seized by a desire to feed the errant cats near your temporary home, you would be making an error for which you may pay a price. Firstly, the cats are not the cats we keep as pets in England. They are by necessity skinny scavengers, who live a tough and semi-wild life. Secondly, you will create a dependency. The Greek cats survive by hunting and picking up scraps from wherever they can. When they are fed, they will hang around waiting for food the next day.

Some male cats may even spray the vicinity (where food was dispensed), to mark it and keep the incoming food for themselves, creating a pungent chemical curtain, which you will enjoy every time you open the windows or step out of the car. So, sad as it may be to see skinny cats, the best thing to do, is either really adopt them and feed them every day, (if you are staying for the long term) or leave them to their errant lifestyle. It breaks my heart to say this, and some will disagree with me, but this has been my experience. Greek cats, like all cats, understand people very well indeed.

The tavern cats know who will feed and who won't, by your body posture and probably even the smell that you give off. Those taverna cats are the masters of the mixed scavenge and dependency lifestyle. Animal charities are doing their best to minimise the plight of cats, by keeping the population under control. It is hard to stop talking about cats once you start, but here, I must leave it for now. So back to the village.

The houses in the villages were originally just put together on what land was available, not to mention materials and labour. Things like privacy, views of the landscape, and space within the house came into play, if at all, only after the basic needs for shelter and warmth were met. The wealthy had more land and could afford to employ people to build better houses, but the poor that moved to the interior of Crete probably had very little in mind, apart from getting to a place of safety away from the various marauding fleets of Arabs, Turks and Venetians or Greek brigands. Once there, there was the matter of the punishing hard work of collecting the stones that would form their simple one-up one-down. They would have to be carried one by one (on a donkey, if you were lucky enough to have one) and then would begin the difficult task of shaping the unyielding stones with simple tools and hopefully making a structure that would keep the family safe from the elements. Modern adaptations of these simple dwellings in the '60s used concrete to replace wooden floors and roofs, leading to the ugly square boxes that are now lying empty in so many villages. Later more sympathetic restorations have exposed the stone walls and used wooden beams and tiled roofs, thank God. One can still see the clear division between the lower floor dedicated to keeping the livestock and the upper room, which served as the main sleeping area for the family.

Of course, there are still great swathes of time, when nothing stirs in the village, namely between noon and 4 pm. If you are not partaking of the local habit of sleeping at lunch, this is a time for the quiet-loving souls to do things, but with proper protection from the searing summer sun.

Eight

Driving West at Sunset

Paleocastro as seen from the west

I drive west, still thinking of my time with my brother. We had an impromptu lunch at his lovely home of stuffed vegetables *(Gemista)* and a nice chat. It was a special interlude and I felt rested and happy. I had no intention of doing anything other than to drive back to 'our' village which lies towards the east and is a fair distance from Heraklion. Instead, something compels me to drive in the opposite direction and hopefully a little adventure. I intended to visit a little monastery that I love.

My first surprise was only a minute's drive away, under a long and dull motorway bridge. Paleocastro or Old Castle. This is one of my favourite bits of Venetian engineering on Crete. A few kilometres west of the capital, it just blends into the rock face and simply defies logic. I have always admired it. Today I decide to follow the sign to what I discover is an absolutely stunning beach beneath the cliff face. Only locals were swimming there, as no tourist would ever think there would be such a diamond of a find under a motorway bridge.

Warning: If you decide to visit, however, and you meet a man who tells you there is a nice path up to the ruins... don't listen. He is insane. Oh, and once up there, put your pride aside and crawl down on your arse. Also, should you decide to follow his advice and take the precariously positioned crumbling cliff-edge path, bring a Bible or equivalent holy book and pray. Pray hard

as you descend, and for pity's sake don't look down. Lovely view,
a frightening sheer drop.

Once I had climbed and entered through the vaulted entrance
that is the only part that still stands, I was confronted, once again
with the sheer brilliance of Venetian architecture.

I climbed the granite up to what must have been the first floor
of the fort. It is built in a diamond shape, its sharp corner an

extension of the cliff face. It stands there, the two outer walls facing east and west, its perfect corner like a ship's bow. Quite marvelous.

I drive on for another 30 minutes, and I am now convinced that I missed the sign to my intended destination, when suddenly there it is. When I set off on the way to the monastery, I could not recall with any accuracy the distance from Heraklion. I somehow remembered it to be just around the corner, but it was in fact a fair distance away, and my little drive took me into the next prefecture.

The Monastery of Attali or Bali, is built on the hill of Agia Ypakoi, west of Bali, with panoramic sea views to the sea and close to the main national road connecting Rethymnon to Heraklion. The region was isolated till 1970 and monastic practice flourished until the construction of the highway.

The monastery of Bali is dedicated to St. John the Baptist. The complex is built on two levels. As I enter the complex, I see a middle-aged monk on one of the benches. He appears lost in thought, as he looks at the sprawling landscape beneath us. I guiltily take a photograph of him. It is unusual to see a monk in the main visitor space.

There was apparently a heavy door guarding the only entrance to the complex. It is doubtful, looking at the layout and the height of the walls, that a gate could have stopped an onslaught, but one must remember that when it was built, there would have been steep rocks and hardly a path to be seen.

With the construction of the motorway and the monastery becoming of interest to visitors, a narrow winding singletrack has been built leading to the site. The Bay of Bali was one of the key points for supplying the rebels with ammunition and for communicating with liberated Greece.

Turkish troops tried several times to occupy the area, causing severe damage to the monastery. In Sifnos, there exists another eponymous Bali monastery, which is believed to be the place where the sacred icon of Our Lady was transferred to protect it from possible destruction.

I have visited the monastery a couple of times before, but this time, the wooden door leading to the upper level was unlocked. I ran up the narrow stairs and wandered quietly in the beautiful narrow courtyard, formed by the narrow blocks of the monk cells and a room labeled 'Trapeza' which means 'table' or 'bank'. There are large stone arches joining the sides of the living quarters. The colours of the materials have aged beautifully and the doors and windows are framed with suitable plants that can withstand the dry summers.

I took some time just looking at how the weather had mellowed the colours of the stones and the plaster and looking for clues about the monastery's history. Parts of the upper block had collapsed at some point and although these did not detract in any way from the sense of order, I wondered why they had not been restored. I spent a long time looking at the surrounding mountains and the view in front of the little garden that frames the church. Then, as it was nearing closing time and everything had been secured, I reluctantly descended the steps back to the car park and drove back to the motorway.

There cannot be a nicer view that greets you as you descend down from the monastery of Ioanni Prodromou (St. John the Forerunner). The vast expanse of cerulean and cobalt blue sea of the Bay of Bali and beyond is held like a baby by the massive range of the Talea Mountains.

Continuing my way down the winding single path, I see the monastery handyman's van precariously parked near the sheer drop. He is sitting above the chasm, his feet dangling over the edge, smoking. He turns to face me, and I am too absorbed by my thoughts to greet him in time, and I continue down to the motorway.

As I re-joined the newly built road, I realised that I did not pick the best time to drive west. The sun is descending fast, and the road is beginning to glow like a river of bright, blinding gold.

Nine

'I Looked Inside'

I looked inside

This old heart

And there the river

Still ran

And everything

Was full

Of you.

It was a hot day, but luckily there had been cloud cover, and as the day drew to a close, the air began to feel cool and fragrant as it drifted over the mountain herbs that hugged the rugged landscape. I took an unusual turn on the main road, and I found myself parked next to an old Agricultural Commission sign. On a weathered map, I could just about make out some local species of birds and a path leading to the river.

I decided to take the little dirt track, and within a few minutes, I was amongst old olive trees and allotments that must have been thriving some thirty years ago. Their borders lay clearly delineated in big riverbed stones. I realised that place was, in fact, the deep ravine that I saw each day on my drive along the mountain road. I had been told stories by the locals of thriving water-driven flour mills down there and had fleetingly glimpsed parts of stone walls on the brink of collapse.

Suddenly, there it was. A huge, powerful river that had coaxed and rolled and dragged millions of huge, rounded stones down its course. The locals had referred to the river as flowing so strongly, "it would take your head off" if you were not looking. The surprisingly big riverbed was dry. It lay there silent and obsolete, straddled by an ancient Roman bridge. The loss of the river suddenly hit me hard. Up above me, a few kilometres away from all natural water sources, had been redirected to an immense reservoir designed to supply the local towns. The village nearby was now as dry as a bone. Its name, meaning 'Riverside' is redundant.

The dry, deserted landscape filled me with a desire to hold on to what was left. Despite being a recent arrival to the area, not a local, I become angry, sad, and emotional. It seemed as if the very life of this land had been wrenched from it, yet people carried on and continued to hope and toil in these harsh conditions. I sat beneath the gnarled olive trees and allowed these negative emotions to run their course. Momentarily I sensed my heart swell with a feeling that was hard to place or measure. It was love for all that is fleeting, human and vulnerable in this world. When back at the house, I drew this little heart-shaped image.

My love for this land, the people and my family had found a sort
of expression. I created this drawing, which I dedicated to them.

If you look closely, you can see the submerged village of Sfondili,
another casualty of the dam. In my mind, this work flies against
life's disappointments and catastrophes; the image is about love
and hope and, more love. Faced with the inevitability of loss
made me feel that the ones we love are truly precious.

Ten

Moonlight in the Mountains

In the distance, in the far distance, the bark of a dog. Then, nothing. Utter silence. This lack of noise, the stillness of the night, opens you up and focuses a heart like nothing else. The moon is almost full. Thank God. Any fuller and it would make you cry. How can something be so beautiful?

The moon, bright as day shines intermittently through ink blue clouds. It plays a silent hide and seek, more for the sake of propriety than fun. Every glimpse, every curve of the circle an aching joy. 'Here, look, hey you, human; yes, you: this is heaven. Have some, look, the light: honey, mother's milk, first love's kiss, gold and silver, hope, eternity, freedom'.

And you.... drive. The road is long and the turns are unfamiliar, after a long absence. To the right a sheer drop, and to the left the steep mountainside. The moon is ethereal, a silent caress. You are still firmly held back in your material 'now'. The physical world tugs you back. 'Remember who you are: Driver, father, tired, anxious, mind full of stuff'.

'Let go... Home is not a place but this light that shines and whispers to you: Everything is fine, let go'.

Eleven

Acts of Kindness

We arrived with a spectacular bump at Heraklion airport. The plane was rattling like a toy train for the last stretch, and it put my minor worries in perspective. We are like fragile fluffy stuff on an extra thin silk thread and life can summon up an f***** major storm at any second. So why sweat the small stuff?

But oh my God, I was so glad to be here. Collected the car from Hertz, an absolute dream with a few hundred miles on the

clock. The woman that served me was so kind. She sustained
eye contact, all the time. It is the cultural norm here. A small
thing but big, in fact. She spoke of her daughter who loves art.
I was relieved. I tried to make conversation on the plane, but it
is hard when folks won't engage. Absolutely fine, of course, but
what lonely lives people must lead, without the capacity to talk
cobblers to one and all when the opportunity arises. But what
a blessed relief, landing and being here. One could never feel
lonely on Crete unless you tried extra hard; people just want to
talk. They somehow think that talking to a stranger is magical,
worthwhile, and interesting.

The drive to Potamies was heavenly. The motorway was mirac-
ulously finished, illuminated, and signposted to the max, and
weaving through the mountainous terrain in the dark seemed
almost fun. The village, even in the cloudy moonlit peekaboo
light, looked beautifully clean. I dropped my car keys and bend-
ing down to retrieve them, I noticed how clean our little street
was. Swept, washed. Stubbornly cared for by the village council
and the neighbours. It is an act of kindness towards everyone
who lives here.

A saintly someone had lodged lavender and rosemary in the
little gap of our front door. It was dry but fragrant. Someone
wonderful had planted geraniums in an old huge plant pot on
the side of our house and had been watering them. It made me so

happy, that I felt completely at peace and glad to be here. I am still full of joy; that small act of kindness invigorated me completely.

The house had been sealed for a year and little creatures had moved in. Spiders in the downstairs window and little beetles by the front door. The house smelled of quiet repose, and thankfully not neglect, and all the bedding was fragrant from the lavender I had packed between the sheets and pillows.

Nothing inspires me more than simple kindness, nothing can match that. After a day of swearing and reality drama, Wonder Woman pilot, saving the day, and chili-con-carne *à la* Jet2 (only £12 with a glass of *Sowd-Afriken* cabernet sauvignon) it is the geraniums that got me. Small acts, big loves. Simple really. Goodnight world. The day begins early here. Donkeys, cockerels, itinerant salesmen with blaring megaphones. Small drawback: no lie-ins are ever possible in Cretan Villages.

Twelve

'Gedling'

Some footprints are indelible.

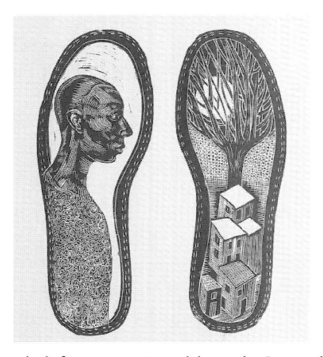

Engraved relief print on 1960s work boot soles. It seemed like
a simple idea, but it clearly went beyond the ordinary. I post-

ed the engraved soles and the imprint on various social media platforms, where the reaction was in some cases extraordinary. Maybe it touched something beyond the inventiveness of using a previously unused surface as the printing plate? Perhaps. Or perhaps it was a quiet day on social media.

I like the image for its powerful simplicity and the mixed messages it communicates. Shoes are both symbols of journeys and yet they are also defiled by the act of being trodden on. They are destined to walk on the ground, picking up the dust and detritus of the sidewalk. They are unseen, these neglected soles. Despite that they are essential. They form the base of our physical being. They protect us from harm. They are both unimportant and indispensable. Under these shoes, the neglected and downtrodden soles suddenly became 'art'. I liked the dichotomy, the dialectic of this juxtaposition.

I had some old late 1960s synthetic under soles from work boots, a remnant of the days when things like that appeared in my studio and sat there waiting for the perfect moment. It seemed to me that after the events following the death of George Floyd, a kind of mass catharsis started to take place on social media. I have worked in environments where a student's background is of paramount importance to the progress and life circumstances of students. I saw many people I knew divulge their pain and distress, their anger. Hidden stories surfaced. The soles of the metaphorical shoes were exposed. Illuminated. High contrast. Of course, a lot of what was happening had always been there, hidden, menacing, and unseen, but leaving these tracks on the environment, on society, and, of course by inference on individuals, including me.

At the time of writing this post, I was aware that other countries and contexts are even more problematised than the UK. Trump's rhetoric of hate and division had at the time formed an obnoxious cloud cover, camouflaging anger, racism, and frustrations; allowing them to come to the surface and challenge decades of hard-won, small but important changes in behaviours and attitudes. The United States for example. Trump's subsequent defeat at the polls has allowed this vile miasma to be less oppressive, and less backed by political power, ignorance, and neglect. I write with at least a lighter heart, but I am not feeling secure yet.

I too was left with a feeling of having suppressed memories, for the sake of getting on with my life and in order to function. I was also surprised to find that when people spoke of difficult experiences, I could relate, despite the fact I had in fact been given many opportunities and had been very fortunate professionally. My life and circumstances are, one would say comfortable and blessed. Yet, that niggling feeling of the accumulation of unchallenged microaggressions that for four decades were swept under the carpet, the painfully ignorant statements of good intent the underlying xenophobia, the awkward silences... all came knocking. No life is ideal, but a life lived in some fear for your well-being, whether emotional or physical, leaves marks.

It was in that spirit that the 'Gedling' relief print was carved into the work boots, as a reminder and an echo of my time living in Gedling, in the early '80s, a place that still referred to itself as a mining village.

The print is about those cold winter mornings when walking to college, I had this feeling of being the 'other'. Of the 'other' being unseen and downtrodden. Or the whiff of impending violence, made by conflicted heavy, honest, hardworking boots, thumping down hard on the floor of the mine and once on me. The ugly flats near St. Mary's Avenue should have been pulled down long ago. They remain as they were, devoid of beauty, stark and unfriendly in the grey of winter. Yet, another conflicting emotion arises in me, as there in those flats, my parents knew true friendship from a kind and warm couple. They unlike the flats have now left us, for what I sincerely hope is a nicer place, with a prettier view. The tree and moon are my parents. The relief in the drudgery, the hope amid the concrete.

The appearance of the figure on the left panel (the right boot sole) is not a reflection of me, or anyone else, but it is a symbol of what I felt whilst relieving some of the verbal and physical confrontations that sadly marred my late teens. We lived in that little corner of Nottingham, resplendent with a beautiful church, lovely vistas of farmland, and the river Trent. I recall the carefree bike rides (moving too fast for the bullies to shout obscenities) towards Stoke Bardolph, the enviable manicured lawns of the less congested areas that enveloped in greenery these older houses near the river. They changed as you rode back uphill towards St Mary's Avenue into rows of ugly 70s-built flats and small awkward post-war semis. There, I, a newcomer to the UK, learned that being a 'European' means nothing if that is not the way people see you. It really is a harsh yet important lesson in self-perception and identity.

I learned that you are fair game to bored and aggressive teenagers in the street, or fellow 'enlightened' Digby College students (and occasionally staff) who would use any opportunity to use painfully racist language to hurt and exclude you. Sometimes to punish you. Other times, as a casual amusing retort. By coincidence, one of the perpetrators, quite oblivious to the harm and distress he caused, recently wrote to me cheerfully on social media. 42 years later, I have not forgotten, what for him was probably just another casual act in an otherwise unremarkable, college day.

As I worked my way through the British education system and was blessed with a position of some authority, I often wondered how anyone in education could allow such blatant aggression to go unchallenged in an environment where young people experience the turmoil of adolescence. Do the perpetrators of racism recoil from those memories? Do they I wonder find a way to simply ignore their unresolved past, when as in the aforementioned man's case they become 'enlightened' enough to befriend me now?

I feel harsh making these judgments about another time and another place. Yet, from an early age, I also recall not wanting to hurt others and belittle them. Maybe that aspect of human behaviour, that of knowing that you can hurt others is relatively free of social norms? In other words, hurting others is not acceptable in any historical period. This is a big topic, I know. Such expansive thinking whilst making such a small print. I judge that to be a good sign, often leading to thought-provoking work.

Remarkable the power of the footprint, and those tracks that last much longer than expected.

Thirteen

'Jimmy's'

I am sitting at a Costa coffee house having a cortado. I drink this frothy drink because it is a small beverage of coffee and froth. Unlike the other gigantic and gut-bloating concoctions on offer, this is just enough of a drink without the gaseous aftermath of a cappuccino. The young woman who served me made a beautiful little drink. On the froth is a sweet little flower. My toasted cheese sandwich is also lovely. Fresh and hot. Maybe a little bland, but quite perfect. A small, beautiful oasis of corporate food and coffee. A place for those of us who are self-employed and can regulate the start of our day and avoid the weekend crowds.

I grew up around a more leisurely way of life on a Greek island. For the last 40 years, living and working in the UK made cafe culture feel alien and unnecessary. Indulgent. A bit lazy. That feeling is hard to shake off, although I know how hard Greek people work. Funny thing, conditioning, and habit. And cultural stereotypes. If not, we absorb them and we reflect them back at ourselves and others. I am sure that I have over-compensated for this image of southern Europeans, working longer and harder than I needed to.

So, anyway, there is not enough space here to explore this, so back to today's theme.... I am looking over the road at the new 'Grill-Seafood and Sushi' restaurant. Ambitious, I think. Imagine being the chef there. All those hygiene rules and all that cross-contamination to consider. I relax knowing that they would have thought all this through and all will be quite exemplary in that respect. The man who works there, perhaps the owner, is looking at the uneven flashing above the glossy black and orange sign, with a big prawn. The prawn has something like steam rising from it or the graphic equivalent of steam. Over the sign, on the first floor, a beauty parlor is advertising painless exfoliation and laser hair removal. I look for the door to the first floor and can't see it. Must be around the side.

The man all in the standard black shirt and trousers is having a fag. He looks a little anxious. He solicits a response from what seem to be passers-by and engages in a discussion about the sign. I am taken back to a time last summer when another man was serving us seafood on the beachfront in Crete. He had been doing that for the last thirty years. I wonder how long this guy, all in black will last. I feel a sense of sadness and injustice, that his surroundings are not as inspiring, but more than that, I feel a sadness that his job will not be celebrated in the same way as the Greek guy's.

It is common in Greece to be served by the same person all your life. There is no stigma to being a 50-year-old waiter, you see. Perhaps it is not the most desirable profession, but it has a lot of positives going for it in that culture. Socialising is the norm. Staying at home in the evening is not. Being a waiter is hard work, but it is not as draining within a culture that thrives on social relationships and where being around people is not seen as exhausting, or stressful. Climate, of course, plays a big role, and it is harder to motivate yourself to go out of the house on a bleak midwinter evening, to eat or meet up with tired friends.

Climate is key to the way we interact and defines a lot about our social life and our character it seems. Whatever the reasons, working in the service sector is both less stressful and culturally more acceptable and desirable in a country such as Greece, as opposed to the UK. Tourism is a lucrative seasonal addition to the mix, which allows for long respites in the winter, so this is another part of the equation.

A Greek psychoanalyst Mathew Josafat spoke of the South to North European differences in character. He observed that Northern European counseling sessions tended to focus on the workplace and work-related matters as the sources of stress and dissonance in most cases where clients seek support in a psychoanalytic setting. Southern Europeans and Greeks, according to him, did not focus on work as their primary stressor but instead concentrated on themes involving people, friendships, and family relationships.

Back to Jimmy's new business. I felt a tinge of sadness for 'Jimmy' or the man in black. His surroundings are the main road, heavy traffic, other small businesses, a local Tesco, a Red Cross shop, and student accommodation. Nothing wrong with any of those things, they are just simply not the same as uninterrupted views of the sea. He is going to work hard to keep this business going and he might not find his efforts appreciated quite as much as his Greek equivalent, but even if he is appreciated, he might see this as a short-term career, not his life's work.

I returned to my cortado. It was lovely. The waiter and waitress were new. I had not seen them before and I guess given the fact that such jobs are not seen as long-term career choices in England, it may be the last time I will see them. Shame, I thought and looked at 'Jimmy' stub his cigarette out and return into the darkness behind the smoked glass of his restaurant. I really hope he makes it work.

Fourteen

From One Friend to Another

It is hard to discuss painful things with friends and those that we love. It is also very hard to find answers for those wonderful people in our lives who are suffering from debilitating illnesses.

We have all been ill with something or other, and we know the helplessness that can permeate our whole bodies... and minds, even with something like a bad cold!

Writing like this can sound glib and over-simplistic, especially when someone we love is seriously ill, so I hesitated, should someone confuse this with medical advice or a way of treating or attempting to deal with a terminal illness? No, the purpose of writing this is to help what can be helped.

I start with the premise that depending on what ails one, there lies a little solution, hopefully somewhere on the continuum of the vast array of things that can go wrong with us all.

Despite my reservations and the caveat that everyone is different and that this is not advice, just my personal contribution to an eternal debate... I want to talk about things that affect us, things that can be hard to overcome, such as a sense of futility or helplessness that can accompany a depressive illness. Sadly, it is a lonely affair, where the things that we need (i.e., help and support) are the very things that we deny ourselves. I have worked in this field, and I know that it really is the loneliest of ailments.

Depending on the severity of the illness, treatment and solutions must be actively sought. It has been described to me as a feeling 'of sinking in quicksand'. A good friend who has lived with this for a long time has been kind enough to tell me more about a way of coping, which resonates with me and I am sure will sound familiar to a lot of people. I am eternally grateful to my friend for being brave enough to share this with me and for allowing me to summarise and publish it here and on my blog.

I had a sense of sinking in a vast pool of quicksand. I struggled to get out of it, but it felt impossible to free myself from the feeling that all I wanted to do was just let myself be enveloped and drift off, somewhere, anywhere. I was at a low point and in pain. Then I began to think of all the people around me that I cared for, that cared for me... and all the people that I had yet to meet and love. The future was a place of fear, but I decided that I wanted it anyway. I wanted to know what would happen. I knew from where I was that there was a better place. It was then that I made a decision, not to 'disappear' from my family any longer. I think they must have felt that I had already gone to a different place. I had stopped communicating and lived in a permanent state of feeling lost and a victim to this way of feeling, this depressive cloud.

I knew that staying still and not fighting against this wave of sadness was not an option. I had to change something before anything would feel different. So, I did. Some ten years ago, when I made this decision, I was self-medicating with various substances. I was a professional victim and opted out of living and of feeling as much as possible. I was also watching myself losing my place in this life. I wanted to live, to be free of this, to breathe and grow.

I stopped all my addictions, big and small over time, over many months in fact, but it was my realisation that any change had to be self-imposed that saved me. I slowly started to eat better. To exercise, to be kind to myself in my thoughts which had always been self-deprecating and hurtful. But what came first, what I knew I had to do, was 'doing'. Just doing things. It was painful rejoining the human race and it was hard getting up and facing my fears every day.

Going to work after an absence of six months, was the hardest. I wish I had done it earlier because it really felt like another vast unfamiliar universe when I returned to my workstation. My body was tense, and I was anxious, and I was aware of my heart racing and my head spinning at the size of the task. I kept on. I sought help from my doctor and colleagues that I could trust and over time I became a little more awake and more willing to take life as it came. It took a long time, but now as I look back, I feel a sense of relief, of having escaped a prison that was not of my making, but which I had unwittingly colluded with.

My advice to anyone who can relate to this is to seek help but expect to have to work hard too. I am grateful that I feel all that I feel, good and bad. This is me. This is what life is, and I accept it. I embrace it and I am not afraid of it any more. Although everyone is unique and your situation may be vastly different, I hope this brings you some hope. Working to free me from my prison was the one thing that I really had to work hard at in my journey to self-acceptance and to living a life that felt good.'

Fifteen

The Gift of Old Age

In this painting of an old man, I was exploring the use of acrylic
paint to create the appearance and particularly the chiaroscuro

effect in an 'old master'. I was not disappointed with the out-
come; it is as they say, what it says it is.

Acrylic paints, certainly the way that I have always used them,
as less forgiving than oils. They can have a harshness and lack
of translucency and of course, they dry quicker. The last part,
which causes problems for many, is the reason I adopted them as
my medium of choice. It is possible to use acrylics to complete
several layers of a painting in a day. I used to think that that was a
great advantage and, in some ways, of course, it is. This painting
and its textural appearance would have taken me days to achieve
if I was working in oils.

Although this was primarily an exercise in the use of a particular
medium, it nonetheless has a story to tell. No painting is without
a personal narrative, either 'built in' by the artist or superim-
posed by the viewer. People have asked me if this is an old version
of me. Although this was not my intention, it is without doubt,
as all paintings are, a kind of self-portrait, a kind of vehicle for
expressing something about the human condition.

I was inspired by some of Rembrandt's portraits, but this went,
as often pictures do, in its own direction and assumed a persona
that I could not have foreseen. I look at this picture now and in
it, I see modest contentment. Not the gloating of a self-satisfied
man, but a time of quiet celebration.

Old age, which as a younger man I believed was an affliction, I now recognise as a gift. Living a long and healthy life is something desirable, but it is not a given. Old age is not to be pitied, rather than to be celebrated. Sure, there is a loss of vitality and youthful exuberance, but in a way that too has to be a welcome development. As we move through life, we are under pressure to create, to make a difference in the world; if we drive our body hard, as I have, it is a relief to see that some things are no longer on the menu, so to speak. Walking for hours at a time? Not so appealing. Running a marathon? Just seems like a few miles too far... Feeling tired more easily? Great. Time to read, sit, or reflect on things in a less frenetic way. We see more when we travel on a slow train.

I think that good emotional health involves an acceptance of change; to be precise, change that we cannot control. An accommodation, even a celebration of sorts. It is great not to always be in the driving seat. When we are young, there is huge pressure to feel in control of our 'destiny'. Many of these things, the drive to change the world, and to provide a better future for our children through our endeavours, are praiseworthy. After all, we have to live as if we are going to be around for a long time, otherwise, we might as well give up. I do not want to lose sight of that, or dismiss the importance of feeling eternal, whilst we have the advantage of youth and when we still feel that time is on our side.

If we were to dwell on the inevitability of death, we would surely wither away. Perhaps we need a new paradigm for ageing and passing on; a convincing social shift, not just a religious afterlife, not just something that people of faith can share. Perhaps this is a discussion that will happen as we look at other paintings.

So then, feeling that we have forever, that life is going to be long and productive is what needs to happen so that we can build and create and leave a legacy for others. What I am saying is, that as we age, we perhaps need to acknowledge a little at the time, that life is time-limited. That we as beings really only have one day at a time. Yes, we need plans, but we must let go of control.

I do not pretend to have all the answers. In fact, the reason that I am writing this is to help me find some. To help us all find some.

So why is the painting important in terms of self-discovery, self-disclosure, and in terms of creating meaning?

Well, any painting reflects several significant factors back at the artist: technical skill, inspiration, and personal meaning. The viewer picks up on some of those, or not, or if we are lucky, embellishes some of them with personal layers of meaning. This painting says the following to me: I can create this image, after many years of practice, yet the complete sense of achievement and translation of a thought into an image, is still eluding me. The skin tones and textures are adequate, and some might even see them as accomplished. For me, they lack the intentionality and clarity that true masterfulness brings; so I have some way to go.

The man in the picture has led a long and interesting life. He is possibly well-educated, has had a family, and has traveled. Life has not always been easy, and he has had his share of sadness as well as happiness. Perhaps he is thinking that he could have focused more on happiness during his life, perhaps the bad times need not have taken so much of his free time. Old age does that for some; it makes them process losses, dwell on past disappointments, and harbour needless pains of things that no longer matter. The man in the picture is beginning to think that maybe he should feel a sense of achievement and pride at a past lived as best as circumstances allowed. A joy in having been there, rather than regret that he was not perfect.

So, the painting is autobiographical after all. I would really like to think that this man is me, twenty years from now (God and the universe and my genetic code willing). This painting is a silent tool, passively reflecting our inner world back at me. You, the viewer, will see something which revolves around your belief system and view of the world, and you within it. I am acknowledging that a painting sends us signals from our subconscious; signals which we may or may not recognise.

Talking about the painting explores this aspect of subconscious reflection and makes us truly think about the messages that we sometimes contain and seldom analyse fully. That is the therapeutic aspect of art. Art criticism, which I have always found tiresome, is a form of therapeutic intervention. Who would have believed it! Oh, did I mention that old age affords us the opportunity to challenge long-held beliefs and to re-frame our points of reference?

Thank God for the time and for being well enough to see old age and really appreciate the insights it brings.

Sixteen

Pandemic

We often think of the birth of a new child with joy, but also with
an attitude that betrays our lack of awareness. To be born is not a
simple thing. It is not without danger, and it is always a miracle.

No matter what the creature is, this is possibly the greatest event of them all. It is the thing that breaks the membrane that separates consciousness from non-existence if you like a bit of poetic license. Some are aware of lasting for a relatively short time unless one subscribes to an 'afterlife'. On that note, religion, once a safe place, is scary to me now.

As I write this, there are 7,794,798,739 people on the planet. Precisely at 16.09 on the 27th of April 2020, there were 258,522 new births, and a few minutes later 108,961 souls departed this mortal coil. (It took me a while to get that last sentence almost right). In reality, they are really just being converted into a different form of energy. We are all sensitive about death and all equally overjoyed at new life, so all this information is given to set the scene, not to diminish their importance. Each loss and each gain is immeasurable, because the human heart, despite its minuscule size in cosmic terms, is in fact the only thing we have that can hold the infinite wonder of love. And true love means transcendence. The extension of one's soul beyond the self, into the unknown of another being's worldview. Love is sacrifice, beauty, and awareness of what really matters.

Many lives end too soon, and some do not get to live. In Charles Dickens' Great Expectations, the young Pip describes the graves of his five brothers, who all died either at birth or soon thereafter: ''To five little stone lozenges, each about a foot and a half long, which were arranged in a neat row beside their grave, and were sacred to the memory of five brothers of mine - who gave up trying to get a living exceedingly early in that universal struggle - I am indebted for a belief I religiously entertained that they had all been born on their backs with their hands in their trouser-pockets, and had never taken them out in this state of existence." Infant mortality rates have improved in some parts of the world, but still. Being born is a dangerous thing and it involves luck, biology, and some other bits of random chance.

Since 2020, we have become more aware of our mortality. At the original time of writing some of the short stories, we were under lockdown. We now know that a great many thousands die each day and that our existence on this planet is more precarious than we cared to imagine, well, acknowledge. We talk of the great open spaces of our planet, of freedom, the expansive nature of the oceans, the endless skies... But these things are comparatively very small and what's more, they exist in a closed little system, a tiny sphere that floats in a vast universe. All these facts and all these happenings will someday form a short paragraph in a set text in a secondary history class somewhere in a school rated to be 'just about safe enough to attend' or whatever the terminology of the future will be.

It seems a fitting time right now when human existence can be seen more clearly as vulnerable, accidental, and precarious, that a single life should come into sharper focus. Each one of us is asking some existential questions. Some are small and some are big, and the difference between them can seem both vast and negligible, depending on when you ask, who you talk to, and what you believe in. The time of day is also important. Never ask someone before their first cup of tea in the morning, as the answer will be incomprehensible.

Seventeen

Fellow Passengers

As must be obvious by now, I occasionally write something whilst waiting for flights at airports. I am not usually short of inspiration and time passes slowly when you have finally navigated security.

This time around, I am struck by the number of people that are waiting for mobility assistance. I was feeling a little jaded until I passed by the dedicated bay. It is near a Deli sign that reads 'Monster Fully Loaded Onion Ring, Mayo, Sausage and Egg Half Loaf'. In smaller playful text beneath it, a further qualifier of this culinary wonder: 'Think Titanic'. I am pondering the mindset that created this enticing pre-long distance flight digestive challenge. I ask myself if the unfortunate reference is intentionally humorous. I conclude that it is an error of judgement.

But it is the crowd of my fellow pre-boarders that draws me in. I am quickly brought up short for my dour demeanor and blasé attitude to travel. Even more so, for taking for granted my ability to still trundle unaided up and down the airport, laden with duty-free goods, feeling bored.

A dozen or more travelers, all looking splendid in crisp, bright summer clothes are waiting patiently in a dedicated bay. They are temporarily parked it seems, on a variety of mobility chairs and scooters. They appear without exception to be (unlike me) full of life, giggly, chatting, and exchanging jokes with airport staff. A gentleman in his 80s with a huge toothy grin winks at me as he is being pushed along in a wheelchair by an airport attendant while his partner struggling on stiff hips (I imagine her joints clicking like mine) heroically navigates the crowded corridor of our tiny regional airport. I am impressed by her stoicism and her use of an elegant walking stick. I fantasise about a bespoke walking stick of my own, if and when my time comes to adopt one. I come back to reality.

A younger woman in an electric mobility scooter rushes past. She too looks stunning in a dress with a striking sunflower design. Two couples are boarding my flight, pushing their partners in airport mobility chairs. I feel humbled and inspired, chastised and grateful, aware once again of the inevitable approach of old age, the possibility of needing support from others to get from A to B.

I ponder for a moment what I would do if I was in a wheelchair. I seriously doubt that I would be so brave as to navigate a crowded airport and fly for many hours. Not to mention the endless preparations, the unpredictability of public services both here and abroad, and the sheer effort of it all. I ask myself if I would be big enough to accept help. I realise that I am oversimplifying here, in my brief glimpse at airport life. I know from professional though not personal experience, that lack of mobility is a hard and challenging path, made harder by society's often flagrant disregard for those with diverse needs.

I suddenly feel guilty for focusing disproportionately on my elderly co-travelers and those needing assistance and I look up to read the minuscule screen announcements.

The lady opposite me is reading a book titled 'A Positively Final Appearance'. I try to avoid overthinking it and open a bag of mini Mars bars I bought at duty-free as a gift for a friend's children. Won't hurt them to eat more healthily I muse as I think of my dentist and wince.

Eighteen

Accountable Spaces

I was fortunate recently to connect with the talented author
and academic Chrissi Nerantzi over our shared interest in family
histories. We were having a discussion concerning 'Safe Spaces'
and expressing one's difficult processes.

She introduced me to a wonderful article by Elise Ahenkorah, a
consultant who works with organizations to build equitable
team dynamics and inclusive workplaces. The article "Safe and
Brave Spaces Don't Work (and What You Can Do Instead)"
felt like another missing piece in a lifetime of trying to figure
out several things, namely relating to personal comfort and ease,
friendships, and relationships.

*A brave space is a space where participants feel comfortable learn-
ing, sharing, and growing. Brave spaces are inclusive of all races,
sexes, genders, abilities, immigration status, and lived experiences.
Brave spaces highlight the importance of being brave enough to
enter spaces where you can be your authentic self and share personal
lived experiences. In short, brave spaces are exhausting.*

I read it, nodded to myself, breathed in and out, and suddenly I
was not the only one to have felt these emotions. Not the only
one who has gone on to tell himself off for being too sensitive,
for overreacting; for not being sufficiently robust to ignore some
of the seemingly minor events that have over the years made one
withdraw from certain people and situations.

The article unexpectedly made me think back to a creative col-
laboration with an art organisation early in my career. Our lives
had converged briefly at our first teaching job in the same school
in the 1980s. We met up again a lifetime later to collaborate on

a commission for a public space. I was excited to hear someone else's ideas, so different from my own and to undertake the creative process as a team, rather than solo. I was looking forward to learning and growing as an artist. I saw the possibilities of my practice growing, and becoming a real career. Of course, the euphoria was short-lived. We had different life experiences and that was fine. We did not agree on everything and that was fine. However, we saw social inequalities and structural issues related to race from different perspectives.

I parked my concerns and threw myself into the project. Two months into the work, I started feeling that something indefinable had happened to create a dissonance. I looked through old emails, examined my motives, and looked for anything that I may have contributed to the situation, namely a feeling that we could not communicate effectively about the work we were creating. Yep. It was there. I had started to withdraw. I had played my part and surely it was all my fault. I carried that guilt ever since.

Then the article came along and reading it I had an epiphany. It was not my fault that I had begun to feel uncomfortable. We simply did not have what was needed when people commit to working together on something as personal as making art. Some of my colleagues did not understand the driving force behind my art, the links with my life experiences.

My collaborators were not to blame. They were all well-informed, socially aware, and to the left of centre in terms of politics. They were warm, caring people. However, all this did not place them in a position to truly see and understand my work, and what was perhaps the hardest thing to accept is that they framed my life experiences within the context of 'life is difficult and we all suffer.' We had many discussions about these matters, but not enough time before the project deadline to effectively come together and speak the same language. We appeared temporarily stuck where we were, unable to reach out and help each other to walk in tandem.

I went back to the article recently and many aspects of that experience, that discomfort, began to fall into place. I highlight some things below that enabled me to reflect on what creative partnerships could work for me in the future. Please read the full article, it really is worth it:

Brave spaces negate the daily bravery of equity-deserving communities and provide little value to those who must carry their bravery into a space intended to support them and their lived experiences.

This is where accountable space guidelines shine...but understanding that aligning your intent with action is the true test of commitment.

Accountable space guidelines allow for allies and marginalized communities to agree on a set of actionable behaviours/actions during the discussion to show allyship in real-time and after the event. It allows participants to align their well-meaning intentions with impact through a collective set of guidelines.

So, my friends and I completed the project. I learned a lot from them and I am still learning, as this blog post hopefully demonstrates. I am now left with a strong conviction and a greater understanding than I had previously. Art is far too personal, far-reaching, and dare I say it... fragile (at least in my case) to thrive in a partnership that does not share the same values. It is also too important to expect it to just happen regardless. Yes, of course, art will survive, art will be made in the most difficult, even life-threatening circumstances. But, I am not referring to that here. I am talking about creative partnerships, and the need to choose people to work with, who can 'see you'; acknowledge you; value you, whom you trust, and okay... let's say it plainly: who accept and acknowledge your pain.

In an ideal world, I would really like to commit to working in accountable spaces where all participants align their well-meaning intentions with action.

Nineteen

The Ottoman Graveyard

When I was a little boy, I used to love digging in the garden of our house in the suburb of Mastampas *(Μασταμπάς)* near the city of Heraklion in Crete. I had read about being an archaeologist in one of the Disney annuals that had a special feature about the subject. It resonated with me and made my digging around seem worthwhile. I dug incessantly. It was a real joy to finally have a garden, having spent the first few years of my life in an apartment in the city. I loved the garden and somewhere, not sure where, but somewhere very safe, I still have an album of cuttings of the trees and plants of my Cretan Garden.

Most of my finds were bits of coloured stones and the odd shell. Sometimes, but very rarely, there were tiny fragments of bone and one day a rather large bone, which I ran to my mother with. My mother did not seem particularly impressed and said it was probably an animal bone, perhaps a remnant from a distant barbeque. I think I was convinced that it was something extraordinary, but Mum knew best, so it was promptly returned to the hole and a new excavation site was begun close by.

It was some decades later when I was researching the Arab Emirate of Crete (827-961 CE) that I was prompted to look into this matter in greater detail. 'Mastaba' I discovered is the Arabic word for bench or a mudbrick superstructure above tombs in ancient Egypt from which the pyramid developed. I also found that an Arab coin was found near our house *(Provenance: Mastampas, Crete. Museum inventory number 1832. Examined in September 1961).*

The island of Crete was apparently a multicultural hub and until 1913 was not even part of Greece. Later an Ottoman graveyard was located in the same place. I am now convinced that my discovery was a human thigh bone. I imagine the spirit of a Turkish man looking down benevolently as a little child innocently uncovers his remains.

Twenty

The Miraculous Encounter

Manolios was walking slowly and deliberately across
the quiet path that led to the edge of the village
from the allotments. A man in his mid-thirties and

a keen loafer, he sported the clothes unshaven face and physical demeanour acquired after many years of strategic inactivity. He was dressed in his trademark farming clothes of faded blue dungarees an orange sunhat and huge wellies.

He was a little nervous and he made his usual little throaty sounds, which were the cause for his nickname in the village: 'Choiros' (male pig). He was not happy about the nickname nor the connotations, but sadly this annoying habit amongst his many others, was so deeply ingrained, that he simply could not stop. Indeed, just a few minutes earlier, as he passed by Kyria Katerina's small farm, he had an uncontrollable fit of grunts, while she was trying to explain to him that one of her prized quail had gone missing from its cage.

He expressed his heartfelt regrets and asked if it could have been a ferret or a cat, or a fox, or... 'a pig?' said Katerina's daughter mischievously. Mother and daughter giggled uncontrollably. He scowled at the little dark-haired girl, but immediately regretted it. Manolios had no evil in his heart. Nor in his large head, wherein a large expanse of empty space one figure stood, sturdy and robust and womanly in a way that Manolios admired, and at times feared.

He left Katerina and her daughter in much better spirits than they had been earlier, and on he went, until he came to Maria's allotment. It was one of a dozen or so, all identical to an outsider; but not to Manolios. To him, the small patch of land, with its orderly rows of cane supports and even a wind chime, was the epitome of order and loveliness. 'Oh, that woman was a marvel. Where did she get all these fancy ideas? A wind-chime!' he smiled, shaking his barrel-sized head.

Manolios often fell asleep with the allotment on his mind and woke up dreaming of Maria tending the plot, her apron tucked into her belt, exposing a bit more of her legs than usual, and at special times, even her amble hirsute belly. It was at times like these, when he had been watching her for quite some time, waiting for just that moment, that Manolios blushed so hard, that his face really hurt, and his *zonari* (cloth belt), seemed to get very tight indeed.

He slowed down as he approached as if to pay this agrarian masterpiece its due respect. Although truth be told, it was not respect that had brought him out at this unearthly hour, nor the much mulled-over image of Maria herself; it was in fact, Maria's tomatoes. They hung in huge numbers from the vines, all gleaming red and unfeasibly large. The morning dew formed tiny tears of moisture which further accentuated their engorged flesh. He instinctively licked his lips, as the large pendulous tomatoes came into focus and appeared to approach him, and not the other way around.

He stopped and took a guilty look at the adjoining fields and the little road. Nothing. It was all still, apart from a distant cockerel and the little wind chime that swung in the languorous stillness of what promised to be another glorious day. He reached trembling over the feeble netting that delineated the allotment from the road and grabbed a titanic tomato. He pulled gently and it quietly yielded its considerable weight into his rough calloused hand. He held it for what seemed an eternity but was in reality a fraction of a second. He found himself salivating at the anticipation of biting hard into its silky cool flesh. He consciously stopped him-self, determined to make this special moment last.

He felt his eyes well up with tears of joy as he held it, turning it to examine the gleaming globe, a whole world of guilty pleasure, right there, in his hand. The stork, the smell, the little cleavage formed by the strained curves. He felt like a pow-erful *effendi* (a ruler) no...even more like the Pasha himself. No pleasure could be denied him. He, the mighty Manolios took his bounty, like a true ruler. Resistance was futile, for all the world was his. He was now slightly cross-eyed at the particular juncture in his world of fantasy and his body and mind had entered a state close to rupture. He was quickly brought back to the reality of the guilty here and now, as he caught sight of a figure ambling towards him.

Unthinkingly and full of remorse and fear, he quickly squeezed the gigantic tomato into his large, dirty pocket. Coming towards him, was Papa Vangelis, the village priest and a man that Manolios had feared all of his life. Papa Vangelis, as well as mak-ing the whole village quake like condemned sinners in his sermons, also had a remarkably heavy hand, which he liked to exercise on the young of the village.

In his youth, a particularly zealous hands-on ear-pulling incident involving a 'naughty boy' (he had not been able to finish the Creed at Sunday school) had caused the local police to pay him a visit after Matins. Of course, no charges were pressed and the policemen also took it upon themselves to tell the boy off, on account of the boy being 'a liar' and 'a wimp' and wasting valuable police time and slandering a 'man of God' and being a right royal pain and so it went on. The policemen had been called out when they could have smoked their unfiltered cigarettes down at the local *kafenion*, which served as the centre of forensic excellence for three local villages. There they dispensed their priceless political wisdom and tipped their oversized hats at the young women who passed by on the way to the small bakery. After a while, the priest magnanimously dismissed them and dropped all charges, but demanded a small payment from the boy's parents for his 'demonic insolence and intentional religious ignorance', in the form of poultry and sausages.

Manolios felt a sudden urge to visit a latrine, as he desperately fought to adopt a nonchalant air of innocence and normality. It was impossible. He felt himself shaking and sweating profusely at the thought of being caught stealing from another villager, not to mention that the particular villager (oh my God, she was bound to find out) held his heart and soul in her plump, gorgeous little hand. Disappointing her was tantamount to losing everything. Manolios' world was crumbling like a *paximadi* (a dry whole meal rusk) being trampled under a heavy boot.

He looked at the frowning face of the priest, his huge bulk waddling in the dusty path, his black oily cassock flapping menacingly, like a bat's wings. Manolios expected a tirade of abuse, even if, he had not been seen stealing the tomato, for the good priest believed that everyone was a sinner, a dirty worthless sinner, and as such should be humiliated whenever possible. Papa Vangelis yielded his powerful voice as a weapon and his cutting remarks were dispensed freely and as a matter of priestly duty. Father of course picked his victims well. With the well-to-do, he unfurled his full-on syrupy

tongue, waxing lyrical and wishing them the protection of the Lord and eternal heavenly loveliness.
Instead, and to Manolios' utter stupefaction, the Father greeted him in a low incomprehensible slur and
continued the waddle towards his allotment.

Manolios was so relieved at this spiritual event, this
glimpse of Papa Vangelis' humanity, this... miracle
that he let out a deafeningly loud greeting which
sounded more like a shrill bird call or a pained
high-pitched squeal. This sudden outburst caused
Papa Vangelis to jump as far as a man of his weight
and level of fitness could challenge gravity. He trun-
dled a bit sideways and then regained his balance
and looked positively petrified.

Manolios' eyes were suddenly drawn to the priest's
tall black hat which stirred in a most peculiar fash-
ion. Papa Vangelis had reached for it with both
hands and was now holding it tight against his rud-
dy forehead, forming a deep sweaty red line. His
considerable girth was still swaying in slow motion,
as waves of cassock-concealed fat were coming to
rest, having been thrown into turmoil. He waddled
down the dusty path at a pace akin to a man running
with his legs tied together.

Manolios watched the figure get smaller and fainter as the waddling priest shuffled down the dusty country path. He scratched his head, and then carefully reached to feel for the tomato, which strained, trapped inside his pocket. He sighed as he stroked it, his calloused hands snagging the fibres of the rough cloth and then carefully, with an imperceptible limp, he too headed for his house as fast as he judged he could walk without a tomato-related incident, and the pleasures that awaited him.

Epilogue

I am not sure now if this was worthwhile for you the reader. Certainly for me, re-reading this collection was a pleasure and at times a challenge. Some things made me smile once again and others, well, they made me reflect on various sad events in my life. Making this book also reminded me that there are good ways to express our feelings and deal with our frustrations. I only hope you felt the same but I guess I will never know. In any case, thank you for reading my thoughts, and good luck on your onward travels.

About the Author

George Sfougaras is a British Greek artist and writer based in the UK. His work is concerned with the way people's lives are affected by history and how national symbols, myths, and rhetoric shape identity. Sfougaras was born in Greece to parents who were refugees from Asia Minor and who came to the UK during the 1970s military Junta period. The cultural changes and challenges that he experienced as an adolescent in Britain later informed his educational work in the classroom and in various leadership roles within the British educational system. These narratives form the cornerstones of his work.

Printed in Great Britain
by Amazon

31640772R10062